Original title:
Closed Pathways and Hidden Dreams

Copyright © 2024 Swan Charm Publishing
All rights reserved.

Editor: Jessica Elisabeth Luik
Author: Liisi Lendorav
ISBN HARDBACK: 978-9916-86-190-5
ISBN PAPERBACK: 978-9916-86-191-2

Murmurs in the Dark

In shadows deep, where whispers lie,
Soft murmurs drift beneath the sky,
A secret told, a silence kept,
In the quiet night, where dreams have slept.

O'er moonlit hills, where shadows blend,
The night unveils its hidden end,
Stars above in silent flight,
Guide us through this endless night.

The whispers grow, a haunting tune,
Beneath the watchful, gasping moon,
Each echoing word, a ghostly mark,
Murmuring secrets in the dark.

Elusive Trails

Paths unmarked through forest dense,
With mysteries lurking, dark and tense,
Footsteps fade on mossy ground,
Leaving not a single sound.

Beneath the boughs so rich and old,
Whispers of tales once bravely told,
Shadows flicker, dance, and play,
On elusive trails that drift away.

The winds that sigh with ghostly calls,
Embrace the paths and ancient halls,
Onward still, we roam and seek,
The trail fades with shadows bleak.

The Road Not Taken

Two paths diverged in autumn's wood,
I stood and pondered where I should,
One well-worn, the other clear,
Whispers calling faint but near.

Chose I the road less worn by feet,
With rustling leaves, a solemn greet,
A journey marked by choice and fate,
Closed the sound of night's debate.

As time goes on, and I look back,
Upon that road, carved by my track,
The road not taken still whispers pure,
Its secrets lost, yet hearts endure.

Curtains of the Mind

Behind the veils, where thoughts reside,
Curtains fall and shadows hide,
In corners dim where secrets find,
A world within the restless mind.

In twilight's shade, where visions shift,
Time and space begin to drift,
Dreams pour forth in endless stream,
Through the mind's dark velvet seam.

Each shadow cast by hidden fears,
Each curtain drawn reveals the years,
Through veils of thoughts and whispers kind,
Rise the curtains of the mind.

Invisible Tracks

In twilight's tender, silent realm,
Where whispers dance and shadows helm,
A pathway forms, unseen, untamed,
By dreams and hopes, unnamed, unblamed.

Soft echoes tread on grass and bark,
Invisible their mark, yet stark,
They guide us through the fog and mist,
Toward realms by daylight never kissed.

Each step is light, yet firm and true,
On paths unseen through morning dew,
We find our way by heart and mind,
To places only dreams can find.

Cryptic Trails

Through forests dense, where secrets hide,
On cryptic trails we softly glide,
The leaves whisper their ancient lore,
Of mysteries they've seen before.

Shadowed paths, by moonlight shown,
Guide hearts to places yet unknown,
In silence, steps leave naught but thought,
As cryptic trails our seeking wrought.

The symbols carved on tree and stone,
Speak truths that only night has known,
We walk by faith, our lanterns dim,
Through cryptic trails, to nature's hymn.

Stilled Avenues

On stilled avenues where silence roams,
Through hushed corridors of ancient homes,
A quiet peace, profound and deep,
In whispers soft, the moments keep.

Each footfall gentle, barely heard,
As echoes blend with the unseen bird,
We wander through the ghostly lanes,
Where time and space release their chains.

With tender hearts and open eyes,
We trace the paths where silence lies,
And find in stillness, solace sweet,
On avenues where worlds can meet.

Byways of Midnight

In the velvet cloak of midnight's reign,
We wander down the byways' lane,
Beneath the stars' eternal light,
Through shadows deep, devoid of sight.

Each turn reveals a hidden view,
By moon's pale gaze, both old and new,
The night, a canvas, vast and wide,
Where dreams and fears in darkness bide.

We travel on these silent roads,
Unbound by time's unyielding codes,
And find within the midnight's gaze,
A world that echoes nightingale's praise.

Midnight Reveries

In shadows deep, the night unfolds,
Stars whisper dreams, a tale untold.
Moonlight dances on silver streams,
We drift away on midnight dreams.

Silent whispers, echoes of time,
Memories weave in rhythmic rhyme.
Embrace the stillness, let it be,
A journey through eternity.

In twilight's arms, we find repose,
A gentle touch, a fleeting close.
Dreamers wander through the night,
Chasing whispers of the light.

Veiled Reflections

Mirrors speak with silent grace,
Haunted by an unseen face.
Fragments of a shattered past,
Reflections that are meant to last.

Through the mist, a shadow's hue,
Past and present, intertwined view.
Glimpses of what once had been,
Echoes lost, but felt within.

Beneath the veil, truth resides,
In the depths, where time abides.
Seek the light within the glass,
A journey only hearts surpass.

Abandoned Passages

Echoes linger in silent halls,
Whispers trace the crumbling walls.
Memories of footsteps gone,
The silent song of days withdrawn.

Cobwebbed moments, dusted dreams,
Forgotten rivers, muted streams.
Time's embrace on stones so cold,
Stories of the brave, the bold.

Silent sentinels stand in wait,
Guardians of an ancient fate.
Abandoned yet they still convey,
The remnants of a brighter day.

Uncharted Paths

Beyond the known, the wild calls,
Nature's silent, secret halls.
Steps that lead to unknown ways,
Through fleeting dusk and dawning haze.

Adventures lie in shadows green,
Mysteries slept in places unseen.
Travelling hearts, undaunted, free,
Seek the truths beneath the tree.

Paths untrodden, worlds untold,
Chronicles of the brave, the bold.
Wind and whispers, skies uncharted,
Journeys end where they once started.

Whispers of the Forgotten

In ancient woods where shadows play,
Old echoes murmur of lost days.
Forgotten tales in breezes spin,
Secrets of what has always been.

Leaves rustle soft, a gentle sigh,
Ghosts of memories passing by.
Unseen they drift, in twilight's breath,
Whispers of life that transcends death.

Enshadowed Journeys

In the whisper of the night,
Silent paths unveil their trace,
Beneath the moon's soft light,
Dreams and shadows interlace.

Steps through darkened lanes,
Carry hopes in silent streams,
Echoes of unspoken pains,
Merge with silver-tinged dreams.

A faint but guiding star,
Hangs in the velvety expanse,
Reminds us who we are,
Through the shadows, we advance.

The journey's cloak is thick,
Mistrust snuggled by doubt,
Yet we push through each trick,
Finding new routes, no way out.

Enshadowed paths we tread,
With hearts both true and frail,
Led by a thread so thin and red,
We walk, we rise, we sail.

Muffled Ambitions

In the core of restless hearts,
Eager dreams lie muffled tight,
Quietly they yearn and start,
Wishing, hoping through the night.

Covered by a shroud of fear,
Ambitions breathe a muted sigh,
Though their voice is hard to hear,
They look for ways to touch the sky.

Subtle sparks in shadows caught,
Yearn to blaze, to burst, to beam,
Though they seem but scattered thought,
They're the echoes of a dream.

Bound by whispers cold and stark,
Muted by the weight of dread,
The soul reignites a spark,
And the quiet words are said.

In the hush of hidden strife,
Silent cries no longer bound,
Ambitions leap to claim their life,
In their voice, a soaring sound.

Hushed Ways

In the shadow of the twilight's haze,
Whispers soft in the silent blaze.
Footsteps light on paths unknown,
Nature's secrets gently grown.

Beneath the stars, in humble grace,
A tranquil night, a quiet space.
Wind's embrace, a tender kiss,
Moments lost in timeless bliss.

Soft murmurs as the leaves do sway,
In the stillness of the fading day.
Echoes of a distant past,
In these hushed ways, peace is cast.

Undiscovered Treks

Mysteries lie where few will tread,
Paths unseen, to dreams they're led.
Valleys deep and hills so high,
Beneath an endless, open sky.

Wanderlust in each footfall,
Adventures grand, though whispers small.
Every step a story new,
Worlds unveiled in morning dew.

In the heart of lands untouched,
Treasures find in pockets clutched.
Through the wild, the spirit flees,
In undiscovered treks, it's free.

Covered Routes

Under canopies dense and vast,
Sheltered from the voices past.
Hidden from the world's loud call,
In the veiled, we find the all.

Paths entwined like threads so thin,
Wonders lie just deep within.
Every turn a sweet surprise,
In these covered routes, hope lies.

Shadows dance on forest floors,
Guarding secrets, ancient lore.
In the stillness, truth's colludes,
Life unfolds on covered routes.

The Locked Gate

At garden's end, the gate stands tall,
A barrier, silent, through seasons' call.
Beyond its bars, a world unknown,
A mystery where time has flown.

Rust and ivy, nature's claim,
Guard the secrets, still and tame.
Key of courage in heart concealed,
Unlock the gate, let dreams be revealed.

Quiet Rambles

Silent steps through fields so wide,
Nature's breath, our only guide.
Whispers in the morning's light,
Peaceful rambles, pure delight.

Streams that murmur to the leaves,
Songs of old the heart receives.
In the quiet, we converse,
Life's plain truths in verse by verse.

Wander where the world stands still,
Feel the calm, embrace the thrill.
In these rambles, spirits mend,
Quiet journeys, without end.

Silent Routes of Yearning

Silent routes where hearts do quietly tread,
Beneath the moon, where secrets softly spread.
Echoes of dreams, unheard by worldly ears,
In whispers, they release their hidden fears.

Paths entwined by fate's invisible thread,
Every step, a tale of love unsaid.
Stars align to guide the tender foot,
Silent routes, where yearnings softly root.

A breeze that sings the songs of time gone by,
Silent routes where teardrops never dry.
Hope blooms in shadows, where the hearts do crave,
Desires buried in a love-sculpted grave.

Secretive Voyages

Through the mist of dreams, they softly glide,
Secretive voyages, where desires hide.
Beyond the reach of light and worldly eyes,
In realms untouched, beneath the twilight skies.

Winds whisper secrets, on their nightly prowl,
Moonlit nights, where silent wishes howl.
Guided by stars, these dreams embark,
Secretive voyages, in the dark.

Away from shores where daylight reigns,
In hidden depths, where mystery chains.
Navigating seas of silent sighs,
Secretive voyages, neath hidden skies.

Veiled Destinations

Veiled destinations, in a twilight haze,
Lost in mazes, where the heart's path sways.
Blood-red roses, in clandestine bloom,
Emotions wrapped in a shroud of gloom.

Footsteps echoed in the silent night,
Veiled destinations, out of sight.
Mystery calls from every shadowed copse,
Guided softly by the whispering tops.

Hearts entwined in a secret embrace,
Veiled destinations, a hidden place.
Journeys taken where the soul desires,
Flickers of truth in forbidden fires.

Uncharted Courses

Sailing on uncharted courses, free,
Where the wind whispers of what could be.
Stars above, a map of distant dreams,
Guiding souls on their silent streams.

Oceans vast, where no bounds are set,
Uncharted courses, where destinies are met.
Every wave holds a tale unsaid,
In the hearts of those who bravely tread.

Venturing where no path is drawn,
Into the unknown, from dusk till dawn.
Uncharted courses, where hope is found,
In the endless skies, without a bound.

Veiled Horizons

Through misty dawn, the day unfolds,
A canvas draped in morning gold.
Beyond the veil, dreams lie in wait,
Whispering secrets, tempting fate.

Horizons glow with muted hues,
A world unseen, a path to choose.
Step forth with hope, embrace the light,
For in the fog, new visions ignite.

Shadows of Missed Chances

In twilight's grasp, where shadows dwell,
Regret's soft whispers weave their spell.
Moments passed, now etched in night,
Dreams once bright, now out of sight.

Fleeting glimpses, paths not tread,
Echoes linger, words unsaid.
Yet hope stirs in the quiet air,
For even shadows shift and wear.

Unrevealed Wanderings

In shadows deep where secrets play,
The heartless whispers of the night.
Unseen paths lead souls astray,
From morning's gleam to twilight's light.

Through misty roads and hidden lanes,
Where dreams and fears silently blend.
Silent steps in darkened plains,
A journey where the unknown begins.

The stars above, a cryptic guide,
In realms where time stands still.
Mysteries in shadows hide,
With a promise of a thrill.

Each footfall sings a silent tune,
Of worlds unseen, unfathomed lore.
Under the watchful, distant moon,
They wander evermore.

Disguised Escapes

In cloaks of whispers, masks so fine,
Escape routes veil the secret binds.
The world sees only the defined,
Yet freedom dances in curious minds.

Steps taken hush yet loud with zeal,
Behind each veil, the breath is felt.
A covert glance, a secret deal,
A world where inward truths are dwelt.

Layered masks in quiet parade,
Escape in forms that few discern.
Through hidden paths, minds evade,
The traps that openly they spurn.

Freedom in the quiet escape,
A ballet of the veiled and true.
Behind each mask, a soul reshape,
In worlds where hidden dreams accrue.

Gated Desires

Behind the ornate gates they lurk,
Desires wrapped in chains unspun.
Where passions in the shadows work,
And longings whispered, yet unsung.

The iron bars of fear and doubt,
Hold fast the dreams that dare to rise.
Yet deep within, the silent shout,
For courage in the heart's disguise.

Each lock a test of will and might,
Each key a promise to the bold.
The gates that hide from common sight,
Desires eager, uncontrolled.

Within the guarded realms they burn,
Bright embers in a darkened space.
Awaiting hands of those who yearn,
To liberate with gentle grace.

Unexplored Alleys

In dim-lit paths where silence reigns,
The alleys weave their mystic spell.
Uncharted by the curious strains,
They guard the secrets time won't tell.

The cobblestones, a tale they keep,
Of fleeting shadows, passing dreams.
In whispers soft, the alleys seep,
Into the mind with silent streams.

In corners dark, the echoes lie,
Of steps untaken, stories missed.
An invitation to the sky,
Where moonlight and the whispers kissed.

Unseen, these nooks of hidden grace,
Yearn for the seekers, bold, unbound.
The unexplored in time and place,
Where truths in silence can be found.

Secrets Beneath the Surface

In the stillness of the deep,
Where mysteries quietly sleep,
Ancient whispers softly weep,
Secrets safe in shadows keep.

Layers hide the untold tales,
Beneath the waves and morning gales,
Silent in their sacred veils,
Guarded by the ocean's trails.

Ripples dance on silent lakes,
Caressing stones with gentle wakes,
What lies below no surface makes,
A mirror world that never shakes.

Below the calm, a separate place,
Time stands still within its space,
A world untouched by life's fast pace,
A realm unseen, without a trace.

In the depths, a story lies,
Hidden from our knowing eyes,
A realm where dream and mystery ties
To secrets beneath the endless skies.

Silent Landscapes

Silent stretches of the land,
Under heaven's gentle hand,
Where nature's quiet marks the sand,
Whispering peace across the strand.

Horizons brush with muted hues,
Sculpting skies in tranquil blues,
A serenade of softened views,
Where silence sings and time imbues.

Mountains stand with silent might,
Echoes lost in morning light,
Valleys bathe in shadows slight,
Nature's song in whispers tight.

Rivers weave with secret tones,
Over moss and ancient stones,
Carving paths through quiet zones,
A melody the world intones.

Silent landscapes calm the soul,
In their quiet, we find whole,
A fleeting peace that takes its toll,
Binding hearts in nature's shoal.

Dormant Desires

In the heart's forgotten nooks,
Lie desires like unread books,
Dreams once caught in wistful looks,
Now resting still in hidden crooks.

Embers of a longing flame,
Whisper secrets without name,
Echoes of a past acclaim,
Sheltered from the world's acclaim.

Hope and fear in quiet sleep,
Promises we vowed to keep,
Bound in chains of silence deep,
In hearts where dormant desires weep.

Awake them from their timeless sleep,
Let them into daylight leap,
No longer in the shadows creep,
For life is full, and time is cheap.

Dreams and wishes, hearts' delight,
Rise above the silent night,
Dormant desires take their flight,
Igniting stars, burning bright.

Ghosts of Tomorrow

Shadows cast by dawn's first light,
Haunting dreams of future sight,
Ghosts of days just out of sight,
Whispering through the endless night.

Unseen hands that shape our fate,
Guide us through a shifting gate,
Through realms where time does fluctuate,
To moments where our choices wait.

Echoes of what might yet be,
Haunt the heart with mystery,
Future draped in secrecy,
A dance with life's uncertainty.

Footsteps taken, paths unknown,
Ghosts of morrows yet unshown,
Whispered in a hushed soft tone,
Leading us where dreams are sown.

In the mist of coming days,
We walk among their shadowed ways,
Crafting futures in a haze,
Bound by ghosts of tomorrow's gaze.

Ephemeral Hopes

Dreams spread thin like morning mist,
On fragile wings they dare to fly.
Moments caught in fleeting tryst,
Beneath the pale, indifferent sky.

Promises whispered, shadows cast,
In realms between the dawn and night.
Time's slow march, relentless, vast,
Yet within, our hopes take flight.

Ephemeral, as the stars that fade,
In the glow of the rising morn.
In their dance, a silent parade,
Of wishes new, and those well-worn.

Catch the wind, though bodies tire,
Chase the light, though shadows grow.
For within each heart's desire,
Ephemeral hopes begin to glow.

The Silent Road

Footsteps fall on paths untold,
Echoes whisper through the pines.
Where the future starts to unfold,
In the hush where the heart aligns.

Silent road beneath the moon,
Guides the weary, lost, and found.
In its quiet a haunting tune,
Where solace and serenity blend around.

Miles stretch beneath the sky,
Carved in dreams and ancient lore.
Silent, but not shy,
Holding secrets to explore.

Walk with me in heart's own beat,
On this road where silence reigns.
Find in stillness, life's retreat,
Where peace in every step remains.

Enigma of the Enclosed

Walls encase the whispered dreams,
Silent corridors of thought.
Within these bounds, light softly gleams,
What's lost and found, and ever sought.

Mysteries wrapped in layers tight,
Veiled in shadows, gently paced.
In dim corners hides the light,
Of truths unspun and chance embraced.

In echoes of the silent hall,
Chorus of the past speaks low.
Promises within the call,
Of what we seek and yearn to know.

Through the keyhole, visions peer,
A world unknown, yet close, and near.
Enigma of the enclosed now clear,
Whispers that the heart holds dear.

Veiled Aspiration

In the heart's depth lies a veil,
Of dreams that scarcely touch the air.
Silent aspirations set to sail,
On waves of hope and gentle care.

Veiled within, the spirit yearns,
For a light not readily seen.
Through the murk, the passion burns,
In colors yet untouched and clean.

Beneath the surface, quiet grows,
A force, a dream, a tale untold.
Life whispers what the heart knows,
In shadows soft, where secrets hold.

Reach beyond the misty shore,
Unveil the dreams, set them free.
In each breath, aspiration's core,
Where hope and future gently meet.

Twilight Fantasies

Beneath the shades where shadows play,
Whispers of dreams begin to sway,
Twilight's blush on evening's face,
Invites the mind to a secret place.

Stars emerge in silent flight,
Tender beacons in the night,
Moonlight casts its silver sheen,
On landscapes of a world unseen.

The wind hums olden melodies,
Ancient tales in rustling trees,
Whispers of a time long gone,
Drift with dusk till break of dawn.

Glimmers of a fate unknown,
Lie in twilight's mystic groan,
Threads of fate in twilight sewn,
Spin a tapestry of dreams alone.

With every shade that softly falls,
Twilight sings through nature's halls,
Inviting hearts to dare and dream,
In the hushed, sweet twilight gleam.

Unrevealed Destinies

Paths unfold in shadowed trace,
Destinies walk a hidden pace,
Each step echoes mystery,
In the dance of history.

Veils of fog, secrets shroud,
Future's song, faint but proud,
Hints of fate in riddles speak,
Silent tales the heart doth seek.

Guided by a truth unseen,
Life's obscure and untread screen,
In the shadows, destinies wait,
Unseen paths to contemplate.

Threads of fate spun from afar,
Glimmer like a distant star,
In the dark, they shine and gleam,
Weaving through the endless dream.

Wisps of hope in twilight's breath,
Lead through life's uncharted breadth,
Each moment holds a key to life,
In the quiet, unseen strife.

Footprints in the Mist

In the dawn, where mist conceals,
Silent paths to dreams reveal,
Footprints whisper, tales untold,
In a land where mystery unfolds.

Steps imprint on fragile dew,
Fade away in morning's hue,
Traces left on nature's skin,
Fade as light begins to thin.

The mist, a shroud of history,
Holds within its tender plea,
Echoes of the steps once taken,
In the morn, by dreams awakened.

Soft and gentle, whispers sigh,
Footprints fade beneath the sky,
Moments pass, like wisps of air,
In the mist, they disappear.

Yet each step, a story's thread,
Vivid paths where dreams are led,
Though the mist may erase all,
Footprints echo, memories call.

Deserted Routes

Windswept paths where silence reigns,
Empty roads and lonely plains,
Traces lost in sands of time,
Deserted routes, a silent rhyme.

Whispers in the arid breeze,
Speak of long-forgotten seas,
Roads that led to nowhere bright,
Fade into the depths of night.

Dusty trails, the heart does seek,
Echoes of a distant peak,
Footsteps mark the lone ascent,
In a land where time is spent.

Empty ways, the desert's grace,
Holds no trace of yesterday's face,
Paths unwound and left behind,
Silent as the wandering mind.

In the quiet, stories lie,
Unseen by the passerby,
Deserted routes of dreams and lore,
Await the steps of dreamers' shores.

Sequestered Dreams

In the quiet of the night,
Where shadows softly gleam,
Lies a world of endless light,
Woven in a sequestered dream.

Through the veil of sleep's bright thread,
Visions dance with silent grace,
Whispers in the mind's deep stead,
Guide us through this mystic place.

Fantasies in moonlit folds,
Where time and sorrow cease,
The heart's hidden warmth enfolds,
A realm of tranquil peace.

Memories and distant hopes,
In this sanctuary meet,
The soul with wonder ever copes,
In dreams so bittersweet.

Awake, we find the day awaits,
Yet treasures linger in our seams,
For within night's quiet gates,
Lie our sequestered dreams.

Hidden Corridors

Through halls unseen, the silent footfalls ring,
In corridors where secrets softly tread,
Shadows linger, whispers softly sing,
Of tales and truths long left unsaid.

Beyond the hidden, mysteries unfold,
Walls conceal the echoes of the past,
In every stone, a story to be told,
Of fleeting moments meant to last.

Silhouettes in dusky corners lie,
Guardians of secrets yet to show,
In every turn, a question why,
In shadows deep, we yearn to know.

Veiled passages of time and space,
Where history and destiny collide,
In silent whispers they embrace,
The hidden corridors where dreams reside.

And as we walk these silent halls,
Each step reverberates with lore,
In every echo, a voice that calls,
To seek the hidden, and implore.

Shrouded Expeditions

Through mists and veils, our journey starts,
In lands where dreams and shadows play,
Guided by the compass of our hearts,
In realms where night blends with the day.

Paths obscured by twilight's shroud,
Lead to the unknown, far and near,
Underneath the star-lit crowd,
We face our doubts, our deepest fear.

Lost in forests dense with time,
Where echoes of the past endure,
We climb the mountains, steep and prime,
In search of truths both bright and pure.

The seas of fog, they rise and fall,
As we sail through mystic tides,
In every wave, a siren's call,
To hidden realms where wonder hides.

Endless are the quests we take,
In shrouded expeditions bold,
With every step, our spirits wake,
To tales of wonder yet untold.

Whispered Ambitions

In the quiet chambers of our mind,
Where aspirations softly bloom,
Silent hopes and dreams we find,
Sheltered from the shadows' gloom.

Through the whispers of our hearts,
Ambitions take their gentle flight,
Crafted in the silent arts,
Of day's dawn and the quiet night.

Each desire, a tender plea,
In the stillness boldly grows,
Guiding us to what might be,
As the silent river flows.

In hushed tones, our visions speak,
Of futures bright, horizons wide,
In whispered words, we seek,
The path where dreams and fate collide.

Thus, in silence, dreams ignite,
Ambitions lead us to our claim,
In the quiet of the night,
We find our whispered dreams aflame.

Requiem of Route

On paths worn by weary stride,
Echoes of footsteps coincide,
With memories of a journey long,
A silent, sorrowful, solemn song.

Along the roads where shadows play,
In twilight's soft and muted gray,
The whispers of the past remain,
In eulogies of joy and pain.

Each milestone marks a tale untold,
Of courage fierce and heartbeats bold,
Beneath the stars and moonlit sky,
The trails of dreams silently lie.

With every turn another thread,
Of stories woven, hope widespread,
In crossroads where decisions weave,
A requiem for those who leave.

In time, the road wears down to dust,
Yet memories live where they must,
Forever etched in souls that roam,
In search of comfort, peace, a home.

Hidden Desires.

In the dim glow of twilight's sheen,
Where secrets shade the world's routine,
Whispers of desires untamed,
In silent hearts, they're softly framed.

Behind veils of daily guise,
Dreams unspoken start to rise,
Within the depths, they twist and play,
In shadows where they long to stay.

Hidden from the piercing light,
Burning in the quiet night,
Flickers of a yearning flame,
Too dear, too deep to ever name.

Concealed in moments, silken, sweet,
In clandestine worlds they meet,
Where stolen glances, tender sighs,
Reveal what guarded thought denies.

Though masked by life's relentless stage,
In the heart, they write their page,
Unseen by day, yet brightly gleam,
In the sacred realm of dream.

Veiled Avenues of Hope

Beyond the mist, the future lies,
In veiled avenues, hope's surprise,
Where dreams walk on uncharted streets,
And fate in whispered promise meets.

Under starlit velvet skies,
The dawn of brighter days arise,
Each step on cobblestone of fear,
Carves out a path, so bright, so clear.

Among the shadows, light is born,
Through cracks of night, it greets the morn,
In every breath, persistence shows,
Where strength in silent courage grows.

Through alleys dark where doubt may tread,
The flickers of belief are spread,
In hidden bends where futures weave,
The seeds of hope take root, believe.

In hushed corners, dreams aspire,
With hearts that dare to chase desire,
On veiled avenues, strong and wide,
Hope walks unbound, a faithful guide.

Whispers in Secluded Corners

In the quiet corners of the mind,
Where solitude and musings bind,
Whispers float on soft, still air,
Secrets spoken only there.

In secluded realms of thought,
Where every echo, silence caught,
Words unsaid begin to form,
In shadows where the heart keeps warm.

Between the sighs and gentle breeze,
Life's untold stories move with ease,
In spaces hidden from the world,
A tapestry of dreams unfurled.

Voices low in murmured tones,
In these hushed, secluded zones,
Conversations safe, unseen,
Within the heart's own private scene.

Here, the soul in quiet sounds,
Finds the freedom, love unbounds,
Whispers in these corners soft,
Lift hopes and dreams forever aloft.

Paths Unseen

Beneath the skies of twilight's sheen,
Where shadows dance on fields of green,
Lies a road of dreams serene,
Untraveled, hidden, paths unseen.

Whispers trace the winding lane,
Silent murmurs, soft refrain,
Footprints mark where souls have been,
Threads of stories, webs unseen.

Branches arch like nature's gate,
Inviting all to contemplate,
Journeys vast and moments lean,
On the secret paths unseen.

Hope resides where doubt holds sway,
Guiding hearts both true and keen,
Seek the light in every scene,
On life's mystic paths unseen.

Stars align in heavens high,
Silent watchers, calm, umpteen,
Lighting ways that intervene,
Showing us the paths unseen.

Hushed Echoes

In the still of twilight's breath,
Whispers linger, shadows cleft,
Carrying tales from eons past,
Hushed echoes that forever last.

Through the corridors of time,
Voices lost in rhythms prime,
Every whisper, every sigh,
Renders memories drifting by.

Winds of change through silence break,
Ripples on a tranquil lake,
Memories in soft repose,
In the quiet, hushed echoes.

Haunting notes in moonlight pale,
Stars recount a wistful tale,
Of forgotten loves and woes,
In the timeless, hushed echoes.

Nightly hums of lives once known,
Secrets in the night wind's tone,
Pause to hear how history flows,
Through the ancient, hushed echoes.

Dormant Pathways

Underneath the starlit veil,
Lie the paths we yet unveil,
Dormant pathways hidden well,
In the night's enchanting spell.

Leaves on branches gently sway,
Tempting journeys underway,
Silent trails where dreams commune,
By the calm of silver moon.

Through the silence, whispers call,
Guiding where the shadows fall,
Every step an untold tale,
Dormant pathways to unveil.

Echoes of the earth arise,
Mystic sights before our eyes,
Marked by time's unyielding rail,
On these dormant pathways frail.

Trust the journey, heed the night,
Cross the threshold to the light,
Paths await beyond the pale,
On these dormant, hidden trails.

Silent Steps

Across the plains where shadows creep,
Silent steps the earth doth keep,
Whispers of the past they trace,
Carving paths in solemn grace.

Barefoot tread on ancient ground,
In the stillness profound,
Every step a gentle breath,
Bridges made twixt life and death.

Moonlight casts its silver hue,
Lighting pathways old, yet new,
Silent steps through night and day,
Marking life's unspoken way.

Cloaked in shades of midnight's silk,
Moving soft as morning's milk,
Traces left for hearts to find,
Silent steps, in reverent mind.

Trust the whispers underfoot,
Each step taken, resolute,
Guiding through where darkness slips,
Life's own trail of silent steps.

Barred Avenues

Golden paths that shimmer bright,
Block the way with beams of light.
Dreams denied at gates we face,
Hopes confined in endless space.

Steps we take on roads ahead,
Haunted pathways of the led.
Winds that whisper through the night,
Tales of futures out of sight.

Hollow echoes in our minds,
Seeking roads we cannot find.
Distant cries from paths once dreamed,
Now the sun has bitterly beamed.

In the shadows still we yearn,
For the roads where hearts will turn.
Barred avenues, closed tight,
Hold the whispers of our might.

The Unseen Voyage

Sails unfurled on seas uncharted,
Wind and waves our course have started.
Beyond the horizon's far embrace,
Lies a world we dare to face.

Stars above our guiding light,
Moon that beams through endless night.
Whispers of the ocean's lore,
Calling us to distant shore.

Tides that shift and waters deep,
Guard the secrets they will keep.
Echoes of the mariner's tale,
In the silence we set sail.

Bravery and hearts so pure,
On this voyage, unsure.
Unseen lands our spirits crave,
Through the tempest, we are brave.

Dreams are cast with every wave,
Hopes upon the seas we pave.
In the darkness light will show,
On this voyage, we will grow.

Passages Untraveled

Forgotten trails in forest deep,
Where dreams and shadows slowly creep.
Steps untaken, roads unseen,
Whisper tales of might have been.

Leaves that rustle, branches sway,
Paths undrawn in light of day.
Quiet echoes call us near,
Voices of both hope and fear.

Unknown worlds beyond the veil,
Stories whispered in the gale.
Journeys waiting to be found,
Silence is the only sound.

From the roots that clutch the earth,
Grow the roads of unknown worth.
Passages that twist and wind,
Through the years they'll never mind.

In the heart of forest grand,
Lies a world not touched by hand.
Passages untouched by time,
In their depths, the spirits climb.

Undiscovered Wishes

Stars that twinkle in the sky,
Hold the secrets where dreams lie.
Wishes made in silent plea,
For a world we cannot see.

Shadows dance with soft moonlight,
Hopes unfurl in dead of night.
Undiscovered, yet we yearn,
For the wishes we discern.

From our hearts the whispers fly,
To the heavens, our dreams high.
Echoes of our deepest thought,
In the vast unknown, caught.

Cherished hopes and unseen dreams,
In the night, our spirit gleams.
Undiscovered wishes rise,
In the darkness of the skies.

In each breath a silent prayer,
To the cosmos we declare.
Dreams unbound will take their flight,
Wishes glowing in the night.

Veiled Trails

Beneath the moon's soft, tender hue,
Lie paths unknown, to venture through.
Whispers from the leaves awake,
Mysteries born in night's embrace.

Footsteps fall on hidden ground,
Secrets in the dark abound.
Lanterns light a fleeting trace,
Dreams emerge in quiet grace.

Stars observe from skies afar,
Guardians of the tales that are.
Shadows stretch, elusive, pale,
Guiding us on veiled trails.

Each step unveils a subtle sign,
Boundaries blur, stories align.
In the heart of twilight's gaze,
Mystery and wonder blaze.

Paths converge, then drift away,
In the night, the heart will sway.
On these trails of silent plight,
Hope and twilight intertwine.

Secret Passageways

Through the walls of ancient stone,
Whispers guide, yet paths unknown.
Vines entwine in hidden play,
Secrets guard the passageway.

Beneath the castle's lofty dome,
Echoes speak in secret tones.
Footsteps lost, then found again,
Mysteries in shadows blend.

Candles flicker, shadows dance,
Hopes reside in hidden glance.
Each corner hides a tale of lore,
Guarded by the myths of yore.

In the heart of silence, stray,
Lost within a secret's sway.
Walls confide and then conceal,
Truths that whispers might reveal.

Paths converge in hushed refrain,
Silent watchers, ancient gain.
Endless stories passage through,
Timeless space in secret hues.

Hope resides in shadow's deep,
Guarded paths our secrets keep.
Within these ancient passageways,
Legends born in twilight stays.

Under Veil of Silence

Night descends with velvet grace,
Silence wraps this sacred space.
Whispers float on midnight breeze,
Dreams unfold beneath the trees.

Stars align in silent ruse,
Casting light on hidden muse.
Moonlight plays on shadowed ground,
Lost in quiet, secrets found.

Through the night, the silence speaks,
Carving paths, where moments freeze.
In the stillness, truth revealed,
Under veil of silence, healed.

Curtains drawn on daylight's past,
Hopes and dreams within the grasp.
In this hush, the world defines,
Silent bonds and unseen lines.

Echoes of a muted kiss,
Cherished moments born of bliss.
Within silence, hearts entwine,
Love and time in silence pine.

In the depths where shadows cease,
Find the solace, find the peace.
Under veil of quiet night,
Hearts and dreams take silent flight.

Labyrinths Locked

Walls that twist and wind, unseen,
Labyrinths of thought convene.
Maze of shadows, paths untold,
Secrets of the heart unfold.

Echoes whisper, guiding steps,
Labyrinth of lost concepts.
In the dark, the mind does roam,
Seeking truths to call its own.

Corners turn, the way is veiled,
Truth and falsehood intertwined.
Endless loop of silent walk,
Boundless hearts in quiet talk.

Locked within the maze of mind,
Keys to thoughts are hard to find.
Every turn reflects a past,
Mirror doors that hold steadfast.

In the labyrinth's core, unseen,
Lies the truth, an emerald sheen.
Unlocked gates, concealed deep,
Dreams and secrets softly sleep.

Find the path, the winding way,
Lost within the twilight sway.
Labyrinths hold hearts enshrined,
In the dark, the light confined.

Forgotten Lanes

Where whispers ride on gentle breeze,
Ancient paths beneath the trees,
Echoes of tales long since passed,
In the shadows, memories cast.

Pebbles crunch beneath old feet,
Steps that many once did meet,
Ghostly laughter fills the night,
A fading, distant, heartfelt sight.

Lights once warm by window's glow,
Now a hush where cool winds blow,
Crickets sing their lonely tune,
Underneath the watchful moon.

Dreams linger in the morning's mist,
Fond moments that time has kissed,
Every corner held a smile,
Forgotten lanes, it's been a while.

Softly now, the past unfurls,
In the silence, time's own pearls,
Treasure troves in memory's chains,
Wander down forgotten lanes.

The Sealed Door

Behind the oak, with locks and key,
Mysteries sealed, unseen to be,
Secrets whisper, shadows call,
Hidden past behind the wall.

Rusty hinges, creaks and sighs,
Guarding tales of bygone cries,
Silent witness, standing still,
Keeper of the unknown will.

Dusty realms of hidden lore,
Safeguarded by this ancient door,
Dreams and shadows intertwined,
All left in the past behind.

Who will dare to turn the lock?
Who will hear the whispers talk?
Glimpse the worlds that sleep inside,
Where the long-lost memories hide.

Yet the door remains so firm,
Holds its secrets, keeps its term,
In the stillness, lore abounds,
In the door, the world it bounds.

Crept Ambitions

In the still of night they wake,
Dreams and wishes, futures make,
Silent hope in shadows wept,
Through the night, ambitions crept.

Stars above, their light bestow,
Guiding paths where dreams must go,
Whispers in the silent dark,
Yet in hearts, ignites a spark.

Steps most cautious, feet most slow,
In the quiet, fervent grow,
Visions seen in slumber deep,
Into waking, secrets seep.

Tender hearts and fiery souls,
Minds with unforgotten goals,
Find their strength as morning breaks,
In the dawn, ambition wakes.

Every heartbeat, every breath,
Pushes through the night's own depth,
Towards a brighter, clearer day,
Where ambitions find their way.

Untold Journeys

Paths that stretch beyond the sight,
Lead to worlds of pure delight,
Steps untaken, tales unfold,
Untold journeys, brave and bold.

Maps uncharted, dreams are spun,
Underneath the rising sun,
Horizon calls, whispers near,
Every journey starting here.

Mountains tall and valleys wide,
Oceans speak with rolling tide,
Footprints in the sand are cast,
Moments fleeting, never last.

Eyes alight with wonder's gleam,
Chase the echoes of a dream,
Every step an untold tale,
Through the woods and down the dale.

Paths converge and then depart,
Journeys told from heart to heart,
Each adventure, spirit free,
Sharing stories by the sea.

Latent Vision

In shadows deep, the mind does dwell,
Where dreams unseen begin to swell,
A silent whisper, soft and pure,
Of hidden truths, obscure allure.

Beyond the veil of night's embrace,
A world unknown begins to trace,
The latent vision seeks the light,
Transforming silence into sight.

In twilight's realm, imagination blooms,
In secret corners, magic looms,
A seed of thought, a phantom glow,
Where unformed wonders start to grow.

A journey masked in mystery's guise,
Through hidden realms behind our eyes,
Latent visions, shadows cast,
Unveil the future, free the past.

From murky depths of muffled sound,
Emerges beauty yet unbound,
The dawning light, austere and bright,
Whispers promise, pure delight.

Lost Pathways

Amidst the woods where pathways twist,
Forgotten trails by time dismissed,
Echoes call from roots and leaves,
A history the forest weaves.

The path once trodden, now concealed,
Its secrets kept, its truths revealed,
Beneath the sky of endless blue,
A tale of old, yet ever new.

Among the trees, where shadows play,
The lost pathways begin to sway,
In whispered songs of ancient lore,
Inviting wanderers to explore.

Deep in the wild where hearts converge,
With every step, the past emerges,
Lost pathways found in nature's maze,
Awaken tales from bygone days.

For those who seek with open mind,
The paths of old are close behind,
In forest halls where dreams cascade,
Lost pathways light a hidden glade.

Silent Arches

In shadows cast by moonlit beams,
Silent arches guard our dreams,
Through hallowed halls where echoes play,
Where night meets dawn and fades away.

The arches stand, a timeless grace,
In quietude, they find their place,
A whispering wind, a soft embrace,
In tranquil depths, their secrets trace.

Beneath the stars' eternal gaze,
Silent arches guide our ways,
Through realms of thought, through dusk and dawn,
In their stillness, dreams are drawn.

A bridge between the now and then,
Silent arches lead again,
To places where the heart can mend,
In quiet corners, time suspends.

In midnight's hush, they softly sing,
Of silent arches, timeless spring,
A journey wrought in peaceful night,
Where whispers turn to guiding light.

Distant Glimmers

On horizons far, where dreams reside,
Distant glimmers come alive,
A beacon's call, a hopeful flame,
That whispers softly, calls our name.

Through the mist of morning's breath,
In shadows where the spirits rest,
A flicker glows, a gentle spark,
Guiding through the world, so dark.

Beyond the edge of sight and time,
Distant glimmers subtly chime,
A light of hope, a future bright,
Pierced softly through the veil of night.

In the stillness of the twilight's grace,
We chase the glimmers, find our place,
Each step we take, a closer view,
Of dreams unseen, of visions true.

A journey marked by stars unseen,
With distant glimmers, guiding dreams,
In silent nights, their glow remains,
A promise held through joy and pain.

Dusky Emergence

The twilight whispers soft and low,
As stars begin their nightly glow.
In shadows cast by day's retreat,
New dreams beneath the evening meet.

The moon ascends with silver grace,
Illuminating night's embrace.
Soft murmurs rise from woodland deep,
As creatures stir from gentle sleep.

In gardens draped in dusk's attire,
Each blooming petal holds desire.
The air is thick with mysteries,
Unraveled by the midnight breeze.

Silent steps on cobblestone,
Paths where ancient tales are sown.
Whispers of forgotten lore,
Echo in the night's encore.

As darkness weaves its quiet song,
In places where the brave belong.
A cloak of stars shields dreams anew,
In dusky night's ethereal hue.

Shaded Ventures

In forests deep where shadows grow,
The silent winds of twilight blow.
Beneath the canopy of leaves,
A whispered secret softly weaves.

Through corridors of ancient trees,
Adventures call on whispered breeze.
With lanterns lit by fireflies,
They guide the path 'neath hidden skies.

Each step an echo of the past,
Where timeless memories are cast.
On mossy stones and winding trails,
The heart finds peace where moonlight pales.

In shaded glades where stillness reigns,
The essence of the woods remains.
With every dawn and dusk anew,
The forest holds its darkest hue.

Beneath the branches, stories live,
Within the quiet, answers give.
Of shaded ventures, deep and pure,
One's spirit finds a way to endure.

Dormant Pathways

Upon the silent, sleeping trails,
Where neither sun nor wind prevails.
Lies dormant earth, untouched by day,
In hidden realms where time's astray.

The whispering grass in slumber deep,
Dreams of the secrets shadows keep.
In quiet groves, the ancient might,
Awaits the call of dawning light.

The stones once tread by heavy heart,
Now harbor tales of time's depart.
In every crack and crevice seen,
Resides the ghosts of what has been.

Yet, paths once trodden don't forget,
The memories in darkness set.
For in their sleep, they hold the key,
To yesteryears' lost melody.

With every dawn, potential stirs,
A promise dormant earth confers.
Awake, the pathways yearn to guide,
Those souls who walk with fate beside.

Stifled Passages

In corridors where silence reigns,
The air is thick with old refrains.
Unseen, unheard, the echoes stay,
In hidden corners far away.

Each passageway a dormant breath,
Where whispers linger, facing death.
The cobwebs form a fragile lace,
Through which the past still shows its face.

Beneath the weight of stifled air,
Lies history, forgotten, rare.
Each step resounds with muted cry,
From halls that long for days gone by.

The secrets held in walls so still,
Like dormant tales they silently fill.
A labyrinth of what once was new,
Contained within a muted view.

Yet, even in these stifled bounds,
A trace of life, a beat resounds.
For every silent passage there,
Holds whispers of a past laid bare.

Masking Unknown Futures

In shadows of the night so deep,
We hide the dreams we dare to keep,
A future masked by veils so thin,
The road unknown, where to begin.

Stars above in silent guidance,
Whispers of a timeless silence,
Steps we take in moon's cold gaze,
Chasing dawns of hidden days.

Through forests dense and valleys low,
Mysteries of life we sow,
Each decision, a path we weave,
In destiny, we must believe.

Hopes emerge with each new rise,
Masked futures, veiled in disguise,
As time unfolds its hidden script,
Our fates by moments lightly gripped.

In courage, we will find our way,
Through untraveled paths of day,
Into the future's quiet call,
Together, we will face it all.

Latent Landscapes of Longing

Whispers in the winds that blow,
Through fields where ancient rivers flow,
Latent dreams in earth's embrace,
Longing etched on nature's face.

Mountains high and valleys wide,
Secreting hope in hearts that bide,
Silent songs of far-off lands,
Golden sand slips through our hands.

Distant vistas in our eyes,
Painting skies with hues of sighs,
Echoes of a time long gone,
Latent landscapes drawn at dawn.

Clouds that drift in endless streams,
Guarding still our hidden dreams,
Footsteps fade yet leave their trace,
Longing fills the empty space.

In every leaf, in every stone,
Whispered tales of seeds unknown,
Latent landscapes serenade,
Hearts with longing softly swayed.

Cloaked Paths

Upon the road where shadows lie,
Beneath a star-streaked, silent sky,
Cloaked paths lead wanderers true,
Through the mist of morning dew.

Silent whispers guide the way,
Through the night and into day,
Shaded trails where secrets blend,
Journeys long with no end.

Step by step, in darkness tread,
By unseen hands we are led,
Through the woods and o'er the hills,
To a place where time stands still.

Moonlight dances on the ground,
Silent echoes all around,
Cloaked paths weave a quiet song,
As we journey, headstrong.

Through the veil of dreams entwined,
Destinations undefined,
Winding roads, a thoughtful quest,
Find our hearts in calmness blessed.

Mystic Spurs

In twilight's touch, a spark ignites,
Mystic spurs of endless nights,
Dreams awakened in the glow,
Ancient tales the stars bestow.

Skies alight with cosmic fire,
Pulling hearts with secret desire,
Mystic whispers on the breeze,
Fates entwined with such ease.

Galaxies in vast array,
Leading souls on paths astray,
Mystic spurs of wandering thought,
In the heart, the journey's wrought.

Echoes of forgotten lore,
Timeless beats at cosmic core,
Tracing lines in astral sand,
Guiding us with gentle hand.

In the glow of ethereal light,
Mystic spurs take silent flight,
In dreams, awake within the night,
We soar beyond, forever bright.

Dreams in the Shadows

In the gloom where phantoms blend
Longing dreams take silent flight
Whispered hopes that never end
In the cradle of the night.

Cloaked in darkness, yet they gleam
Radiant beneath the veil
Silent stars in twilight's seam
Telling secrets, they unveil.

Nebulous, they softly call
Drawing forth the dusk-bound soul
Through the shadows, they enthrall
In the whispers of their roll.

In the stillness, they arise
Bearing forth a secret light
Dancing in the starry skies
Dreams that glimmer in the night.

Hidden in the shadows deep
Dreams of wonder, shadows' breath
Where the quiet visions sleep
In the kinship of their death.

Shadowy Realms

In the depth of midnight's dream,
Elusive thoughts begin to scheme,
Whispers float on silent streams,
Casting shadows, unseen beams.

Moonlight glints on secret looms,
Woven in the night's dark rooms,
Paths unknown, where silence looms,
Dancing shadows, twilight plumes.

Softly echoes lost desires,
Hidden voices, whispered choirs,
Flicker, shimmer, fading fires,
In shadowy realms, fate conspires.

Veils of night obscure the truth,
Innocence and bygone youth,
In this realm, no need for proof,
Just shadows painting life's uncouth.

Through the shadows, light breaks free,
Boundless, flowing endlessly,
In those realms where we can't see,
Peace resides, and shadows flee.

Hidden Passages Unseen

Beneath old walls, secrets hide,
Passages that time denied,
Echoes linger, history's guide,
In corridors once dignified.

Steps unheard in silent halls,
Whispers paint on ancient walls,
Time's embrace as time befalls,
Hidden passages where light stalls.

Lamps that flicker, shadows fleet,
Mysteries twixt stone and street,
Paths where hidden tales meet,
In uncharted, unseen retreat.

Darkness shrouded, tales concealed,
Countless stories yet revealed,
Journeys through the shadows sealed,
In passages where fate is healed.

Through the hidden, seek and find,
Veins of ancient, roots entwined,
Paths to worlds unblemished, kind,
In unseen passages, truth defined.

Masked Journeys

Masks we wear on roads unknown,
Faces clad in borrowed tones,
Journeys marked by muffled groans,
Paths we tread, we walk alone.

In the shadows, whispers blend,
Voices masked that never mend,
Journeys start but never end,
Winding roads that twist and bend.

Sight obscured by twilight's haze,
Hidden truths in shadow's gaze,
Walkers lost in endless maze,
Through the masked, we strive and praise.

Journeys taken, memories bind,
Lost and found in dark confined,
In each mask, a soul designed,
Seeking truths in life entwined.

Step by step, we chart our course,
Masked from loss and masked from force,
In these journeys, find remorse,
But through masks, life's greatest source.

Bolted Avenues

Paths once open, sealed with steel,
Roads to dreams that now congeal,
Avenues where hearts congeal,
Locked and bolted, latches seal.

Windows barred and doors are shut,
Far-off hopes in darkened rut,
Time betrays with one swift cut,
Bolted avenues, life's rebut.

Gates unopened, dreams erased,
Locks and chains our hopes encased,
Through these roads, we make our haste,
Bolted tight, our lives misplaced.

Whispers echo in the night,
Bolted paths obscure our sight,
In the gloom, we seek the light,
Avenues to new twilight.

Yet through bolts, resilience grows,
Strength in heart and spirit knows,
Bolted avenues, hope flows,
With each step, a new dawn shows.

Shrouded Kaleidoscope

A prism hides in veils of mist,
Reflections twist and turn,
Color's dance by shadows kissed,
As silent embers burn.

In shifting hues, the secrets lie,
Within this hidden scope,
Whispered winds beneath the sky,
Entwine with threads of hope.

Through cloaks of gray and whispers dark,
A vibrant life concealed,
Each piece a faint, ephemeral spark,
Of mysteries revealed.

Yet gaze too deep, you may not find,
The truth in colors bright,
A shrouded kaleidoscope of mind,
Masked in shadows' light.

In every fragment, tales unfold,
In every hue, a clue,
To secrets dormant, dreams of old,
In a world of every hue.

Obscured Realms

In realms where silence softly falls,
And whispers seek their home,
A world obscured behind the walls,
Of ancient, endless roam.

Beneath the canopy of stars,
Beyond the veil of dreams,
Lie secrets kept in crystal jars,
Where twilight softly gleams.

Eyes may strain, but never see,
These realms so far away,
Hidden truths in mystery,
Where shadows play and stay.

Yet sometimes, in the darkest hour,
A fleeting glimpse appears,
Of hidden realms with dormant power,
That whisper in our ears.

Obscured, but ever-present there,
They wait for those who seek,
To step beyond the world's despair,
And find the answers they bespeak.

Secret Worlds

In corners where the light won't tread,
And shadows hold their stay,
Lie secret worlds in dreams embed,
By night and not by day.

Beneath the surface of the known,
In whispers soft they dwell,
With wonders crafted, seeds are sown,
In each forbidden spell.

Here, time does twist and stories bend,
Transforming space and thought,
Where fantasies and truths defend,
Realms that can't be bought.

Through hidden doors and silent keys,
In silence, they unfold,
Worlds that move with quiet ease,
And secrets yet untold.

Venture forth, oh, curious mind,
To worlds not left behind,
In shadows, there are truths to find,
Where mystery is kind.

Courts of Mystery

In the courts of mystery where shadows dance,
Whispers echo through the ancient stone.
Silent footsteps tread an uncertain trance,
Secrets whispered by realms unknown.

Veils of night obscure the hidden truth,
Candles falter in the chilling gloom.
Mystic runes recount a tale aloof,
Destinies sealed in forgotten tomb.

Eyes unseen, they watch with endless grace,
Guardians of time's untamed reverie.
Figures cloaked in enigmatic lace,
Hold the keys to infinity.

Labyrinths etched in walls of grey and old,
Guarded hallways speak of timeless lore.
Silent symbols in the dark unfold,
Urging hearts to seek forevermore.

Shadows play in realms of grandeur grey,
Their whispers bind our souls with yearning.
Through the courts of mystery we sway,
In search of light, forever burning.

Hidden Pathways of the Heart

Through the tangles of emotion's weave,
Lies a path both fragile and untamed.
In the silent whispers of the eve,
A journey to the soul remains unnamed.

Crimson trails where love and sorrow meet,
Marked by tears that shimmer in the night.
Hidden pathways pulse with gentle beat,
Navigating shadows cast by light.

Unseen routes where dreams and fears collide,
Echoes of a past that longs to stay.
In the chambers deep where secrets hide,
Lies a map to guide a hopeful way.

Softly tread these winding, tender lanes,
Guarded by the ghosts of laughter's past.
Through the heart's celestial refrains,
Love's eternal beacon stands steadfast.

Eyes shut tight, we follow unseen guides,
Searching for the truths that love imparts.
In the hidden pathways, there abides,
The essence of our longing hearts.

Locked Pathways of the Mind

Labyrinthine corridors obscure and vast,
Twist and turn beneath the conscious plane.
Memories locked in shadows of the past,
Guarded by the mind's enshrouded chain.

Mystic gates to insight's boundless field,
Sealed within the vaults of thought and dream.
Hidden truths that reason dare not yield,
Whisper secrets lost in time's swift stream.

Phantom keys to open guarded doors,
Dwell in whispers of forgotten lore.
Echoes reverberate from distant shores,
As the mind seeks realms it wishes for.

Dim-lit chambers hold reflections deep,
Fragments of a soul entwined in haze.
Locked pathways in a slumbered keep,
Hidden fates in timeless, guarded maze.

To wander here is both a gift and quest,
Unveiling layers, finding wisdom's core.
In the pathways locked, the mind finds rest,
Unlocking depths to discover more.

Dimmed Trails of Hope

In the twilight's gentle, fading glow,
Dimmed trails of hope meander through.
Whispers of a dream once bright and bold,
Now lie cloaked in dusk's encompassing hue.

Echoes of a fervent, burning flame,
Softly linger, graced by silent night.
Through the mire, we wander just the same,
Seeking remnants of forgotten light.

Hues of twilight paint with sombre tone,
Paths where promises and dreams lost lay.
Steps we take, though often hard and lone,
Guide us through the veil to break of day.

In the dimness, glimmers softly gleam,
Hope's faint glow persists against the dark.
Serenade of an undying dream,
Breaths of courage found in every spark.

Through the shadows, though the trail is thin,
Faithful hearts will find the strength to cope.
In the night, resilience deep within,
Guides us on the dimmed trails of hope.

Concealed Bridges of Longing

Beneath the twilight's gentle fold,
Where whispers dance, as stories untold,
There lies a bridge, concealed from sight,
A path of whispers, veiled in night.

Soft winds carry, dreams past due,
Yearning hearts, in twilight's hue,
Steps that falter, yet persist,
On these bridges, dreams resist.

Stars above in silent glow,
Guard the secrets, none may know,
Miles apart, yet close within,
Bridges beckon, where love has been.

Silent shadows, linger near,
Echoes of what we hold dear,
Bridges span where we belong,
In whispers of a silent song.

With every step, a heart revived,
Across the spans where love survived,
Through the veil, the bridges sing,
Of longing's path and hope they bring.

Untrod Routes of Yearning

In forest depths, where pathways start,
Routes of yearning, touch the heart,
Untrod ways, where hopes reside,
Guiding whispers of longing's tide.

Leaves they rustle, secrets share,
Winds of time, wander there,
Untrod steps in moon's embrace,
Yearning's mark, a hidden trace.

Stars align, to light the way,
Promises of break of day,
In shadows cast by ancient trees,
Lies the path, to inner pleas.

Journey deep where silence roams,
Find the place where yearning homes,
Through the mists, unseen by eyes,
Routes of dreams, our longing ties.

Every step, untrodden yet,
Paths of yearning, never met,
Footprints fade, but hearts remain,
In the routes of yearning, free of pain.

Chambered Wishes

Within the depths of hearts confined,
Lie wishes chambered, undefined,
Silent echoes of desire,
In shadowed halls, souls conspire.

Loves unspoken, dreams aspired,
In these chambers, time's retired,
Longing's breath, a fervent plea,
For wishes true, yet still to be.

Walls adorned with hopes entwined,
In quiet chamber, seek and find,
Every whisper, every prayer,
Wishes chambered, linger there.

In silent rooms where dreams connect,
The heart's desire, stands erect,
Yearning finds its sacred home,
In chambered wishes, never known.

Closed within but felt so strong,
Wishes chambered, where they belong,
Silent echoes, heart's decree,
In these chambers, love runs free.

Curtained Crossroads

At crossroads where the curtains fall,
Life's decisions, cast in thrall,
Paths unwoven, yet unseen,
Curtained crossroads, intervene.

Choices wrapped in silken veil,
Every breath, a whispered tale,
Forks that beckon, dreams unfold,
Paths where secrets are untold.

Curtains drift, the future hides,
In these crossroads, fate decides,
Heartfelt calls and footsteps soft,
Paths of life that wander oft.

The veils may lift, or shadows stay,
At crossroads where we find our way,
In curtain's dance, a guide unseen,
To the crossroads of the in-between.

In each turn, a story starts,
Crossroads bring us closer hearts,
Curtained ways where dreams await,
In life's crossroads, love abates.

Milton Keynes UK
Ingram Content Group UK Ltd.
UKHW022119220724
445848UK00012B/177